A Gem's Path

Britley Blessitt

Presentation by *BookLeaf Publishing*

Web: www.bookleafpub.com

E-mail: info@bookleafpub.com

ISBN: 9789357442251

First edition 2023

I dedicate these poems to my family, friends, mentors, and anyone who helped me become the woman I am today.

ACKNOWLEDGEMENT

I pray for the days when love is truly cherished, treasured and savored....
Everything is going to be alright... Just hold on....
I want you to live... not because you have to... but because you understand that your purpose is truly DIVINE.....

Sunlight can blind the darkness. Laughter can cure sadness. Love can fuel happiness...

Thank you to the readers, my family, friends, fellow poets/writers, and BookLeaf Publishing. Thank you for letting me translate my voice into my words.

Thank you to the person who taught me the true art of poetry.

PREFACE

I woke up one day, sat at a table,
And wrote
Poetry that resonates with
Myself, others, and the future
Generation.
Savor each line, truly think
About the theme and how
Poetry makes connections.
Thank you for taking time out
Of your day
To read poems that brings me
Joy and gives me strength and I
Hope these poems do the same for you.

Preserved Hope

You are patient.
You are kind.
You are gentle.
You are savored.
You are loved.
You are unbothered.
You are strong.
You are brave.
You are humble.
You are the light in the darkness.

The Portrait

I believe God is the painter,
The obstacles I encounter form the canvas,
and I am the evolving portrait.

You Don't Know Me

You don't know me
  Or my story
You don't know me
Or my destiny
You don't know me
Or the woman I'm going to be
You don't know me
Or my family
I am not a mind reader
We all make mistakes,
So please understand, you don't know me
Or know what I can do
Don't analyze my flaws or failures
And act like you know me
Because the fact is,
You really don't know me or the woman I'm
going to be.

QuickSand

Sometimes I feel like I'm sinking
Here, over there… just everywhere
Sometimes I feel like I'm sinking
Deeper into an abyss of despair.
Sometimes I feel like I'm sinking
Beyond repair.
Sometimes I feel like I'm sinking
And that's never easy to declare.

I Am A Black Woman

5

I am Black.

I am Black and proud.
I am a Black woman.

Black is bold.
Black is strength.
Black is sophisticated.

You Are The Reason Why...

You are the reason why the sun rises,
You are the reason why the birds sing,
You are the reason why the stars shine,
You are the reason why flowers bloom.

You are the reason why luck was created,
You are the reason why the heart giggles,
You are the reason why love exists,
You are the reason why the ocean dances.

You are the reason why Christmas lasts forever,
You are the reason why Spring comes after
Winter,
You are the reason why Valentine's Day is
magical,
You are the reason why I'm so thankful.

The Wind

The wind used to be my greatest enemy,
I leaned forward, it pushed me back.
To be so powerless yet fearless at the same time,
Such pain, such grace, such strength.

It spoke to me so I became speechless,
I closed my eyes to listen to its story,
The wind was alive and looked into my eyes.
It asked me, "Can you really see me?"

The wind and I paused for a second.
I replied, "I see you, I hear you, and I feel you."
My new friend began to dance with glee,
And so did I. Then we gazed at the clear blue
skies.

Thunderstorm

To be in the eye of the
Thunderstorm is as scary
As it sounds.
I begged my feet to move,
They ignored me.
So I stood there frozen
In the aftermath.

Mother Time

There she was,
Staring at me.
She greeted me.
I frowned at her.
The Past inspires the Present,
The Present inspires the Future.
I chose to stay in the Present.
Move forward, never backwards.

Gems

How much pressure
Can you take?
How much would
You put at stake?
To achieve your greatest
Accomplishments.
Who or what are you
Willing to sacrifice?
How much does success
Mean to you?
Tell me.

Angels & Demons

Daydreams, Nightmares,
Angels and Demons,
Come throughout the
Seasons of our lives
For many different Reasons.

Friendship

More precious than jewels,
Sometimes hard to find,
An individual that makes you
Laugh, feel comfortable, smile
Through the good and bad times.

Friendships can lasts years or days,
A strong bond can even survive distant days,
Endless messages, epic adventures,
Phone calls that last five minutes or three hours
Some friends can make up even if the bond
grows sour.

It's okay...

Some days, it is okay
If you do not want to
Dress up, take pictures, go outside, or
Constantly remain glued to your phone.

It is okay if you get frustrated, sad, disgusted,
Overwhelmed, anxious, happy or embarrassed.
Because we are all humans and we all have
emotions.

It is okay to have good and bad days.
It is okay to have feelings.
It is okay to say how you feel.

It is okay to set boundaries.
It is okay to know your worth.
It is okay to say "NO" and mean it.

It is okay to love and put yourself FIRST.

Hear Us Roar

We are not invisible,
And do not try to make us divisible.

One day, we finally spoke up,
So it caused them to wake up.

We preach of our dissatisfactions,
Disappointed by a nation that fails to take action.

They stirred the pot
But can never stand the heat.

Countless events throughout our timelines
Make us always question when it will be our
time
To unite and feel welcomed,
and our ancestors pat on us on our backs and
Say, "Well Done".

The Goodbye, New Chapter

Some people overstay their welcome,
Some people leave too soon,
And the rest don't know whether to stay or
leave.

The truth can sting more
than a bee.
The truth can also be as
sweet as honey.

Memories trapped in time,
Stuck in replay on our minds.
They remind us of what we
Once were, could have been,
Hoped to be, and who we are now.

I found a way to create the life I wanted
Without you.
I must confess, it was doable but not easy.

Overthinker

If I had a dollar
for every single time
I doubted myself,
I would be rich.

Parents

Parents are
Fighters,
Healers,
Protectors,
Guiders,
Teachers,
Hard-workers,
Dreamers,
Mind readers,
Sacrificers,
Creators,
And, of course,
Our favorite superheroes.

Ohana Means Family

Dear ohana,
I love you
To the moon and back.

Heartstrings intertwined as one,
United bonds can never be undone.

I will always be there for you,
You will always be there for me.

Morning Mirror Pep Talk

I am the unstoppable force,
I let my metamorphosis take its course.

To be of undeniable classy guidance,
Epic soul, you already know what time it is.

I am the energy you desire,
Faith transpired,
I hope to inspire.

Organized chaos,
Glossier than your favorite lip gloss.

Flawless creation
Creating a global sensation.

I am the Sun to a rainy day,
I am the remedy to the wound,
Cooler than the drink on your tray,
Sweet reflection, see you soon.

Her

She became a dehydrated
Plant yearning for water she
Would never receive.

The Blueprint

They say dreamers are fools of their own fantasies,
Because they spend most days escaping their realities.
They say doers are the most exhausted people you will ever meet,
Because doers overwork themselves until they barely stand on their feet.
However, I believe in doers and dreamers.
They co-depend on each other.
Before a doer is created, a dreamer is born.
The truth is everyone dreams.
A dream is a blueprint of reality.